HELLO PRESIDENT

THE 25- POINT PLAYBOOK FOR LEADERSHIP

Jc. MURALI DHARAN R.

First love is always special
Likewise, this first book is incredibly dear to me!

Thank you

Amma & Appa

Dedicated to

Henry Giessenbier – The visionary who started JCI

&

To all my beloved Jaycees – The true Changemakers

Contents

Contents

Preface

HELLO my dear President,
Congratulations on stepping into one of the most exciting roles in JCI!

This book isn't a lecture. It is 100 percent my experience - a full year of leading, learning, making mistakes, improvising, and somehow making it through as a Local Organization (LO) President in JCI. These 25 rules (or laws, or survival tips—you may call them what you like) are a direct reflection of my wins and my mistakes.

JCI is a unique place. Most organizations pick a born leader and hand them the title. But here? JCI accepts an *ordinary* person, hands them a leadership role, and lets them discover just how extraordinary they can become. And that's the beauty of it!

Your one-year tenure will teach you more than any business degree from an elite B-school ever will. Leadership here is not just about managing a team—it's about personal growth, business strategies, and handling people who disappear when work is assigned but magically appear for recognition.

This year, you will lead, you will be tested, and you will evolve. So, dear President, buckle up. It won't be easy. But trust me, it'll be worth it.

Bon Voyage!
Cheers!

About JCI

JCI (Junior Chamber International) is a global network of young active citizens (18-40 years) passionate about creating positive change. In over 115 countries it provides leadership training, community projects, business growth opportunities and international networking. JCI empowers individuals to develop skills, build connections, and make an impact. If you believe in leading with action, learning with purpose, and growing with a global mindset—JCI is for you!

We call each club of JCI as "Local Organization (LO)" and the person who leads the club will be addressed as the "LO President". The Presidentship tenure is one year (1st Jan to 31st Dec)

Vision:
"To be the foremost global network of young leaders"

Mission:
"To provide leadership development opportunities that empower young people to create positive change"

To explore more, kindly visit:

www.jci.cc
www.jciindia.in

To begin, begin!

The first step to doing anything is to *START*. Simple, right? Yet, most of us spend our lives waiting—waiting for the "right" opportunity, the "right" time, the "right" people, and the "right" resources. I used to do the same until I realized that waiting like this is equal to RCB waiting to clinch their maiden IPL title. (As I write this, I still hope RCB wins IPL 2025. But let's be real, hope is not a strategy.)

In reality, *the perfect moment never arrives*. The more you wait, the further you fall behind. The secret? Just take the first step. Once you do, the Universe will be shocked—"Wait, this guy actually moved?" And as Paulo Coelho says, it will conspire to help you. The right people, the right ideas, and the right opportunities will find you on the way.

Think of it like a car's headlights at night. They don't show the entire road from start to finish, just a few meters ahead. But as the car moves, the path keeps revealing itself. Life works the same way—you don't need to see the full road; you just need to start driving.

Thinking of launching a business? A YouTube channel? A podcast? A new habit? Overthinking kills more dreams than failure ever will. Just begin, and everything else will fall into place.

You have got only a year to be the LO President. One-year flies. You can't afford to waste it. So, start taking steps. Planning is NOT the key; real hero is the speed at which you are able to execute things without waiting for perfection. Many Chinese manufacturers will send you a quote even before you hang up the phone! That's the speed we're talking about.

I remember attending a start-up event in December 2023, where Mr. Sridhar Vembu, ex-CEO of Zoho Corp, was asked for one key message for founders. His reply?

"The fast (b)eats the slow."

So, what are you waiting for? Start. Now.

Breathe like a CEO!

JCI gave me the opportunity to drape a tie—properly. Before that, my tie-knot had a 5-inch gap between it and my collar, looking like I was wearing a neck brace. A senior member once pulled me aside, fixed my tie, and said, "You're now an LO President, which means you're the CEO of an MNC. So, eat like a CEO, talk like a CEO, and think like a CEO."

That's when I realized leadership isn't just about taking decisions or leading a team. It's about *presence*. Your presence should make an impact, and even in your absence, people should still feel it.

First things first—how you present yourself matters. People will start noticing your tie, watch, pen, shoes, and even your fragrance. Always carry a pocket perfume. You're not just leading a team; you're setting the standard. Dress well, speak well, carry yourself with confidence.

And let's talk about communication. Public speaking isn't just a skill—it's a survival tool for a leader. You may have the best ideas, but if you can't articulate them with confidence and charisma, you might as well be explaining quantum physics to a toddler. Own the room. Always.

Every CEO has a mental coach, a strategist who helps them stay sharp. Likewise, as an LO President, find yourself a mentor—but choose wisely. Pick someone who has not just succeeded in JCI but also achieved something in business. *Your mentor shouldn't just inspire you; they should challenge you.*

So, breathe like a CEO. Walk into a room like you own it. Keep your energy high. And never forget—people respect confidence, not hesitation.

The art of decision making

Indecision is like a buffering video—annoying, time-consuming, and pointless. Often, we hesitate to commit, thinking a "better" decision is just around the corner. But the truth is, most of our energy gets drained in this endless loop of overthinking.

The first rule: *Don't keep your options open forever.* A clear and compelling vision is far better than drowning in choices. Imagine being at a buffet—too many dishes, too little space on your plate. Pick what matters and move forward.

The second rule: Like I mentioned in the previous chapter, having a coach can be a game-changer during tough decisions. But here's the catch—ask only one person. If you ask 10 people, you won't decide; you'll only debate. Seeking opinions is fine but remember—the final call is yours. If things go right, you own it. If things go wrong, you own that too. No blaming the stars, the economy, or your neighbor's bad vibes.

The third rule: Should you trust your gut? Yes—but back it up with data. Decisions based on intuition alone are like playing darts blindfolded. Sure, you might hit the target, but why take that risk? Validate your instincts with facts.

And *once a decision is made, stop revisiting it.* Constantly doubting yourself is like uninstalling and reinstalling an app—it wastes time, and nothing changes. Instead, *raise your game* by committing to your choices.

What if I make the wrong call? Every wrong decision is not a failure, but a future asset—a lesson that sharpens your ability to make better choices next time. The real failure? Not deciding at all.

Bonus tip:

If you're stuck between a "yes" and a "no" and can't decide? Here's the golden rule—*if you cannot decide, it's a definite NO.*

Now go ahead—decide to be decisive!

The power of saying "NO"

President, if there's one skill you must master, it's this: The Art of Saying NO.

I used to think saying "NO" would hurt people. So, I kept postponing decisions, delaying responses, and avoiding uncomfortable conversations. But soon, I realized there's something called *"expectation management"*—and if you don't manage expectations well, your image takes a hit.

Many times, when someone asks us for something, we feel a FOMO (Fear of Missing Out). We hesitate. We don't want to lose an opportunity, offend someone, or be the bad guy. So, instead of giving a clear answer, we delay it. Big mistake.

Golden Rule 1: *Don't make people wait.*

Think of the previous chapter's rule—if you can't decide, the answer is NO. The worst thing you can do is keep someone hanging.

If you say NO upfront, they may feel disappointed for a moment, but they will respect your clarity. If you say YES and then don't deliver, you lose credibility.

People respect firm and clear responses more than false hopes and delayed disappointments.

Golden Rule 2:

"Will try" = *"NO"*

Example: "I will try to come" = "I won't come."

Sounds familiar? We've all used it. But as a leader, avoid it. Be direct, decisive, and clear.

So, practice saying NO with confidence. It's not about rejecting people—it's about protecting your time, energy, and credibility.

And remember, saying NO to something unimportant is actually saying YES to what truly matters!

Master these two magic words

Never ever feel SHY to use these two words – HELP & SORRY

A single act of asking the right help from the right person at the right time can work wonders.

During my installation as the LO President, I made a classic blunder—I forgot to invite a key Jaycee to the event. (Okay, technically, he didn't pick up my call, and I forgot to follow up.) But guess what? He showed up anyway and roasted me in public.

"Oh! You Murali uh!? Don't you know to invite seasoned Jaycees like us?"

For a second, I froze. Then, I immediately said, "SORRY, sir... this won't happen again."

Boom. Just like that, his anger vanished. No grudges, no drama—he just moved on. And till today, he has been my well-wisher.

That's the power of a genuine apology.

Now, let's talk about asking for HELP.

I once needed funds for a project and approached 40+ businesspeople. The first few rejections bruised my ego. The next few irritated me. But the more I asked, the better my pitch became. Eventually, I got what I needed.

Ego and leadership don't mix. As a leader, you are the bridge between the giver and the receiver. And in that bridging process, your ego is irrelevant.

"The cause must always be greater than your ego." Read that again.

So, never hesitate to ask for HELP. Never hesitate to say SORRY.

One opens new doors, the other closes past mistakes. Use them wisely.

Gratitude – the secret sauce

Three months into my leadership journey, a realization hit me like a speeding auto on a narrow street—everything that happens teaches me something. Good, bad, ugly—there's a lesson hidden in it all.

So, I stopped resisting and started asking myself, *"What is this trying to teach me?"* Instead of sulking over setbacks, I trained my mind to think, *"What next?"* That's the difference between leaders who grow and those who just go. Complaining is easy, but a solution mindset? That's where the magic happens!

Here's a pro tip: Visualize what might go wrong before it actually does. Not in a paranoid way, but in a prepared way. If you're organizing an event, think—what could possibly mess up? No mic? Power cut? Chief guest ghosting you at the last minute? When you mentally rehearse, you can tackle problems before they even arise.

And above all, practice gratitude—to people, situations, and even failures. Just one minute in the morning and one before bed, thanking everything and everyone who shaped your journey, and you'll notice a shift in your energy. Gratitude isn't just a feel-good concept; it rewires your brain for success.

Even the worst critics and toughest challenges contribute to your growth. So, say *thank you*—and watch how the universe rewards you!

From Gossip to Growth – Level Up

I've seen it—people booking fancy suite rooms in star hotels, sitting around a conference table, sipping overpriced tea, and... discussing people. *"Did you hear what he did?" "Oh, that guy? Total disaster!"* Hours wasted, egos inflated, and nothing actually gets done.

Gossiping is like a mosquito bite—feels good to scratch, but it leaves a mark. A leader indulging in gossip is like a CEO spending board meeting debating cafeteria snacks instead of company strategy. Never talk about people—talk about ideas!

"Great minds discuss ideas.
Average minds discuss events.
Small minds discuss people"

So, ask yourself—do you want to be a great mind or a *chit-chat committee chairperson?*

Instead of discussing *who did what*, discuss *what you can do next*. Plan impactful projects, build systems, and create change that lasts beyond your term. Sit with your team and chart out your Annual Program Planner (APP). *A well-executed APP is like a solid game plan*—it ensures your team isn't running around like headless chickens.

Also, set up Standard Operating Procedures (SOPs) for your LO. Because let's be honest—every year, a new president comes in, changes things, and starts from scratch. Without strong processes, your organization is basically playing musical chairs. Build systems, not chaos!

So, next time you find yourself in a long discussion, ask: *Are we solving a problem or just talking about people?* If it's the latter—redirect, refocus, and raise the bar!

Choose your circle

There's a famous saying, "*You are the sum of the five people you spend the most time with.*" If that statement makes you nervous, it's time for an audit!

Let's be real. If your circle is full of people who gossip all day (like we discussed in Chapter 7, guess what? You'll soon be an expert in who-did-what rather than who-did-something-useful. If your circle spends time discussing stocks, business, and growth, chances are, your mind will start picking up those frequencies too.

Want to check the quality of your circle? Observe what they talk about the most:
If they talk about ideas, you're in good company.
If they talk about people, run before you get infected!

If your group's favorite topic is "who is dating whom" or "who got drunk last night," congratulations! You are just one step away from running a full-time gossip column. But if your group talks about innovations, problem-solving, and making an impact, you are on the right track.

Your environment shapes your thoughts. If you hang around with five positive, ambitious people, you'll be the sixth. If you hang around with five lazy, unmotivated people, well... you get the idea.

A small hack—surround yourself with people who celebrate life, who prefer happiness over drama, and who value family and business.

Your circle is your silent mentor. Choose it wisely. Or better, create one that pushes you to grow!

Not everyone likes Biryani

For those who haven't experienced the joy of Biryani... let me introduce you to it! - an iconic South Asian dish made of aromatic basmati rice, rich spices, tender meat (or veggies), and the magic of slow cooking. It's a festival on a plate! But here's the catch—not everyone loves Biryani. Shocking, right? Some prefer curd rice, some want pasta, and some just survive on plain toast.

Now, let's talk about leadership.

One of my fellow JCI Presidents once vented to me, *"Murali, I organize so many training programs, but barely 10–15 members turn up! On top of that, I'm the only one doing all the work—no one supports me.*

Welcome to reality! Just like not everyone loves biryani, not everyone joins JCI (or any organization) for the same reasons. Some are here for training, some for networking, some for business growth, and some just because their friend dragged them in. And there's always that one guy who has no idea why he/she is even here!

Your job as a leader is to understand your people. If someone is here for business, don't keep forcing them into training programs—connect them with potential clients instead. If someone joined for fun, make them part of event planning.

Stop assuming what people need—observe, understand, and deliver. The moment you start offering what excites them, participation will shoot up, and you won't have to drag them in.

Leadership isn't about feeding everyone biryani. It's about knowing when to serve a burger, when to offer a salad, and when to just let people have their favorite dessert.

Don't Chase numbers

Never, ever run behind numbers and PR alone.

One of my good friends proudly did 365 projects in his tenure—one project a day! Sounds impressive, right? Well, out of those 365, only one or two had any real impact. His LO members? They hardly benefited at all. But hey, the guy won a ton of awards.

And that's the trap.

When you focus only on numbers, rewards, and PR, you may lose sight of what truly matters—real value. A thousand training sessions mean nothing if your members aren't actually learning. A hundred events are useless if they don't create lasting impact.

Here's the truth: Numbers look good on reports, but impact looks good in people's lives.

It's like chasing butterflies. The harder you run after them, the more they slip away. But if you build a beautiful garden—if you create meaningful experiences, opportunities, and genuine connections—guess what?

The butterflies (or in this case, success, recognition, and numbers) will naturally come to you.

So, don't just chase numbers; attract results. Focus on creating real value. Numbers and PR are a byproduct of good work, not the goal itself.

At the end of the day, it's *not about how many trophies you've stacked up—it's about how many lives you've truly touched.*

Now, go build that garden!

Do ONE thing repeatedly

Every year, JCI LO Presidents take over like a new season of a reality show—new energy, new ideas, and of course, new projects. But let's be honest, most of these "revolutionary" ideas vanish faster than a New Year's resolution. One year, it's a blood donation camp; the next, it's a tree plantation drive, and by the third year, nobody even remembers what was done before.

Here's the problem: we love variety, but impact comes from consistency. If you plant a hundred trees once and forget about them, congratulations—you've just sponsored a buffet for the neighborhood goats. But if you plant trees every year, nurture them, and make it a tradition, you're creating a green legacy that lasts.

The trick is to pick one powerful, meaningful project and make it your organization's signature. Look at the world's greatest traditions—Wimbledon happens every year, the Oscars never skip a beat, and even your mom's scolding follows a predictable pattern. Why? Because repetition builds identity and credibility.

When your LO does the same impactful project year after year, people take notice. Sponsors come back, the community trusts you, and over time, your one project becomes legendary. Instead of scattering your energy across ten small, forgettable events, channel it into one game-changing initiative.

So, before you brainstorm another "innovative" idea that nobody will remember in six months, ask yourself—what's that one project you can repeat, refine, and redefine every year? Start today, and maybe a decade later, your name won't just be on an old JCI directory—it'll be attached to a project that truly changed lives. Now, that's leadership worth repeating.

Consistency wins

Ever watched a T20 cricket match where a team smashes sixes in the Powerplay, racing to 80/0 in six overs, only to collapse like a pack of biscuits in the middle overs? That's exactly how some leaders operate—full energy at the start, then fizzling out like a leaky balloon.

The first month of your LO presidency? You're everywhere—meetings, projects, social media posts with #LeadershipInAction. By mid-year, you're "delegating" (a fancy word for disappearing; some call it "auto-pilot" mode). And by the last quarter? Your WhatsApp status reads: *Busy, only urgent calls.*

The problem? Leadership isn't a T20 Powerplay. Sure, starting strong is great, but what matters is how you sustain that momentum. Ever seen MS Dhoni panic in the death overs? No.

A good leader doesn't just sprint; they know how to run the marathon. If you plan ten programs in your first two months and then burn out, congratulations—you've just played an explosive Powerplay and invited a collapse.

Instead, pace yourself. A well-balanced innings—one where you keep scoring steadily without exhaustion—always wins in the long run.

Your team, your LO, and even your own motivation thrive on consistency. People don't remember a flashy start if the ending is a disaster. They remember a leader who showed up, stayed steady, and finished strong.

So, don't be that team that makes 100 in 6 overs and gets all out for 130. Instead, be the captain who anchors the innings, builds partnerships, and ensures the scoreboard keeps ticking. Because in leadership—just like in cricket—victory isn't about how hard you hit in the first few overs, but how well you play till the last ball. Keep the energy alive and make your year count!

Frugal mindset

Every *LO President starts their term with big dreams*—grand events, premium venues, and a team that works like a Silicon Valley startup. But reality? You're handed a budget that barely covers tea and biscuits, a mic that sounds like a broken radio, and a venue that's hotter than Chennai in May. Welcome to leadership!

Now, you have two choices: spend your year complaining or become a master of *jugaad* (creative problem-solving). History favors the second type. The Wright brothers didn't wait for NASA's funding to build an airplane. They simply made do with what they had and took off—literally!

The trick? Creativity beats capital. Low budget? Negotiate. Low attendance? Market better. No AC hall? Talk to people! One smart LO President approached a college and got their fully air-conditioned auditorium for *free*—in exchange, the college could send 10 students to every training session. *That's* leadership! You don't need a fat wallet; you need sharp negotiation skills.

Look around—street food vendors run entire businesses from tiny carts. They don't whine about five-star kitchens; they master the art of making magic with one stove and a steel plate. That's *frugality with flair*

Instead of sulking about your limited resources, *flip the script*. If you get only a low training fee, turn it into an opportunity—build credibility first, demand higher later. If your team is small, leverage partnerships, sponsorships, and technology. There's *always* a way!

A true leader isn't the one who works with excess. It's the one who makes excellence happen with *less*. The world doesn't remember complainers; it remembers *innovators*. So, stop waiting for bigger budgets—maximize what you have, find win-win deals, and create impact. That's how you lead like a pro!

Be a talent scout

Delegation is like casting for a movie—pick the wrong actor, and even a blockbuster script turns into a flop show. Yet, some leaders hand out responsibilities like a lottery, only to regret it later. Giving finance work to someone who still uses their fingers for basic math? Disaster. Asking a silent introvert to host an event? Awkward.

Great leaders don't just delegate; they *diagnose* before they delegate. Every person has a unique skill set, and your job is to play talent scout. Observe them. Who's great with numbers? Who has the charm to handle PR? Who can manage logistics without turning it into a circus? When you put the right people in the right roles, magic happens.

But here's the catch—sometimes, even after careful delegation, things go south. Your VP-Training vanishes, the LO secretary forgets there's an event, and suddenly, you're in a crisis. That's when real leaders shine. Smart delegation isn't just assigning tasks; it's knowing when to *reassign* tasks. If Plan A fails, don't sit and sulk—move to Plan B (or C, or even Z if needed).

Think of yourself as an IPL team captain. If your star batsman isn't delivering, will you let him waste all 20 overs? No! You'll shuffle the batting order, send in an impact player, and turn the game around.

So, stop playing blind bets with delegation. Read people, assign wisely, and don't hesitate to reshuffle when required. Because in the end, a winning leader is one who knows that the *right* people doing the *right* things at the *right* time can turn any match—or organization—into a champion team.

Document everything

Most leaders run their term like a wedding buffet—everything looks grand on the day, but no one remembers what was served the next morning. Why? Because *nothing* was documented! No records, no data, just blurry selfies and vague memories.

Here's the truth: *If you don't document, you can't measure. If you can't measure, you can't manage. And if you can't manage, forget about multiplying!*

We live in an era where data is the new oil. AI agents, businesses, and even cricket analysts thrive on data. But many leaders still run their organizations like it's the Stone Age—decisions based on gut feeling instead of real numbers. Imagine trying to improve an event without knowing how many attended, what worked, or what went wrong. That's like driving blindfolded and hoping you don't crash!

One JCI chapter once claimed, *"We trained 5,000 people this year!"* When asked for proof, all they had were a few group photos and some Facebook/Instagram posts with *#GreatImpact.* That's not documentation; that's wishful thinking!

Proper documentation isn't just about keeping records—it's about measuring progress, learning from mistakes, and scaling success. What worked? What flopped? What should be repeated? If you don't write it down, next year's President will be as clueless as a first-time traveler without Google Maps.

It's simple:
Keep track of attendees, budgets, sponsors, impact.
Maintain minutes of meetings (because memory is unreliable).
Document projects properly—so future leaders don't waste time reinventing the wheel.

Great leaders don't rely on memory; they rely on *metrics*. So, start documenting like your legacy depends on it—because *it does!* And who knows? Maybe one day, your detailed records will help someone turn your small idea into a global movement.

Nobody cares about your excuses

Let's be honest—nobody wakes up in the morning excited to hear why *you couldn't get things done*. People are busy. They have their own problems. They're not interested in your budget issues, team conflicts, or how the projector refused to work just before your big event. They only care about what you delivered.

But some leaders? They turn into expert storytellers. *"The venue wasn't available... The team wasn't cooperative... The stars weren't aligned..."* Stop. The world doesn't run on excuses—it runs on execution. If you keep giving reasons for why things didn't happen, soon, no one will trust you with responsibilities. Yet, some leaders show up *after* everything is done and dusted with a full-length drama: *"We could have done better, but the team didn't co-operate... The budget was tight... The audience turnout was low because of the weather..."* If you're explaining after the failure, it's not an explanation—it's just damage control.

A real leader doesn't wait until things collapse to start justifying. Be proactive. If you foresee a challenge, bring it up *beforehand*—not as an excuse, but as a situation to solve. Need more hands on the deck? Say it early. Budget looking thin? Raise it upfront. Crisis brewing? Alert the right people. Leaders don't react to problems; they anticipate them. And let's be clear: leadership is not about blaming circumstances. It's about *working through them*. Low resources? Optimize what you have. Team disengaged? Find better ways to motivate them. Venue unavailable? Adapt. Complaining may give temporary relief, but solutions earn permanent respect.

This doesn't mean you suffer in silence. Seek help, but from the right sources—mentors, guides, or experienced leaders. Just don't wait until everything falls apart and then hold a press conference on why it wasn't your fault. No one's buying that.

At the end of the day, results speak louder than reasons. If you consistently deliver, people will trust you. If all they hear are justifications, they'll stop listening. So, drop the excuses; stop waiting for sympathy—start working for solutions. Focus on impact, because in leadership, *it's not about what happened, but what you made happen!*

Stop trying to impress

If your goal in life is to be loved by everyone, leadership is the wrong career choice. Maybe try selling ice cream instead —like Steve Jobs famously said. Because no matter what you do, someone will always have a problem. Too strict? Dictator. Too flexible? Weak. Too ambitious? Attention seeker. Too silent? Invisible. You can't win them all, so stop trying!

Even within your own governing board, some people won't like you. *Shocking, right?* You imagined standing on stage, being admired by your team like a Rockstar. Instead, you find that half of them are debating your every decision. That's leadership.

The key? Never oppose the person. Oppose their point. Disagreements are part of the job, but the moment you make it *personal*, you've lost. A smart leader challenges ideas, not egos. Argue with logic, not emotions. After all, what matters most is delivering value to your LO members, not winning popularity contests.

Look at history—every great leader had critics. If no one is questioning you, you're probably playing it too safe.And safe leadership rarely brings impact.

So, focus on your mission. Ask yourself:
1. Are members getting value from your leadership?
2. Are your initiatives making a difference?
3. Are you pushing for progress, even if it's uncomfortable?

If the answer is *yes*, you're doing fine. Let the noise fade into the background.

In leadership, your job is to serve, not to please. So, stop worrying about who likes you and start focusing on the work. Because in the long run, respect > popularity. And trust me, even if they don't like you now, they'll appreciate you later—when they see the results! History will be kinder to you!

What is your Karma?

Let's be real—most people don't remember who their school captain was. Or the class topper. Or the guy who gave the *"We'll stay in touch forever"* farewell speech. Because *most people* don't leave an impact. Don't be that forgettable leader.

Your job as a leader isn't to just finish your term and disappear like last year's viral meme. Your karma is to create something so impactful that even after decades, people say, "That was the year things changed!" If all you did was host a few events, take some group photos, and hand over the files to the next guy, congratulations—you've officially wasted your time.

Think about it—why do we still talk about some leaders decades later? Because they didn't just *do things*; they built something that lasted. A project, a system, a culture—something that outlived their tenure. That's real leadership.

Now, this doesn't mean you have to create a historical monument in your name. But ask yourself:

1. Will the programs you started still run next year?
2. Did you set a standard that future leaders will try to match?
3. Will members remember your contribution, or just your farewell speech?

Forget short-term applause. Go for long-term impact. LO Presidentship isn't about looking good for a year—it's about making a difference that lasts beyond you.

One day, someone will recall your name—not because you were the LO President, but because you made something better. That's when you'll know you led with purpose.

So, don't aim for just *a great term*. Aim for a legacy. Because a true leader isn't measured by what they did while in power, but by what remains long after they're gone.

Reputation is Fragile

If history has taught us anything, it's that kingdoms didn't always fall because of wars. Some fell because the king was *too busy chasing the queen*. And let's not even start on how money has turned geniuses into fools. Lust and greed have been ruining careers long before social media did.

As a leader, your biggest asset is your reputation. And here's the brutal truth—once it's broken, no amount of PR can fix it. You could be the most brilliant, hardworking, visionary leader, but the moment you get caught in a scandal, that's all people will remember. Your legacy? Gone.

Let's be clear—this isn't about demonizing men/women or money. Both are amazing. But the problem starts when they become an *obsession*. When leadership takes a backseat and personal distractions take the wheel, progress crashes. A leader too distracted by power, wealth, or personal indulgences will eventually lose respect, lose credibility, and lose everything they built.

You might think, *"Come on, people will forget."* Nope. People forget your successes faster than they forget your mistakes. One wrong move, and that's your permanent label. Ever heard of someone being remembered for *almost* being great? Exactly.

So, what's the solution? Discipline. Priorities. Self-control. Focus on what actually matters—your mission, your impact, and the people who trust you to lead. Money and relationships will come and go, but your reputation stays with you for life.

At the end of the day, the choice is yours—do you want to be remembered as a leader who built something meaningful? Or as someone who got distracted and became a cautionary tale?

Think wisely. Respect once lost is lost forever.

Win at work & home

Picture this: You're standing on stage, holding a shiny trophy for *Outstanding LO President of the Year.* The crowd is cheering, your name is in the newsletter, and your leadership legacy is sealed. But back home? Your spouse is giving you *that* look, your kids barely recognize you, and your business account is in ICU. What's the point of winning in JCI if you're losing in life?

Many leaders go all-in for the fame, the recognition, the "Sir, you are an inspiration" messages. But I suggest, it isn't just about impressing society—it's about balancing your personal, professional, and social responsibilities without burning any of them down. JCI will teach you time management the hard way. You'll plan mega events but forget anniversaries.

You'll network with CEOs but ignore client calls. You'll mentor teams but miss family dinners. And by the time your term ends, you might have built an excellent reputation—but at the cost of your business and relationships.

That's not leadership.
That's mismanagement.

In the recent Tamil movie, *Lubber Pandhu(2024)*, the hero, a local cricket star, gets roasted by his wife:
"Ooruku nallavana irukravan lam veetuku nallavana iruka maatan."
(*Those who are good for society won't be good at home.*) That line hits hard because it's true for so many leaders. They give their all to the world but leave their own home and work life unattended.

Here's the trick: Balance.
1. Block time for business, family, and JCI separately.
2.Delegate responsibilities at work just like you do in JCI.
3. Communicate with family—they must feel involved, not ignored.
4. Don't let your passion for service become an excuse for personal failures.

Leadership isn't about just winning trophies—it's about winning trust, stability, and success in all areas of life. Your term will end, new leaders will come, and people will eventually forget your award. But your family and business? They'll stay. So, don't just win outside—win inside too. That's real success.

Keep your enemies close

Let's get one thing straight—if you think there's no politics in leadership, you're either too naïve or too new. Leadership without politics is like cricket without sledging—*it just doesn't exist.*

But here's the catch: You don't have to play dirty politics. You just need the *knack* to understand it. Read people. Observe their moves. Know who's genuinely supporting you and who's just waiting for you to slip so they can take the credit—or worse, take your seat next year.

There will always be *that one person* in your governing board who subtly opposes everything you do. If you say, "Let's launch a new project," they'll say, "But we've never done that before." If you say, "Let's continue an old project," they'll say, "Why aren't we thinking of something new?" Basically, their full-time job is to make your job harder.

Now, a weak leader sees these people as threats and avoids them. A smart leader? Keeps them close. Involves them. Gives them responsibility. Makes them feel important. This way, you're not just neutralizing their opposition—you're making them work *for* you. Turn your enemies into fans using the right knack.

So, the next time you spot an "enemy," don't push them away. Bring them in. Keep them near. Because the closer they are, the easier they are to handle. And who knows? By the end of your term, they might just be clapping for you.

One word can change a life

A round of applause. A simple "Well done." A small certificate. You have no idea how powerful these things are.

People don't just work for money or titles. They work for attention, appreciation, and affection. Even the toughest, most no-nonsense person melts when recognized in public. Want proof? Just call someone onto the stage at an event, hand them a memento, and watch them transform from "I did nothing" to "I dedicate this to my team" within seconds.

Recognition is a *game-changer*. The more you appreciate people, the harder they work. The more you honor their contributions, the more they contribute. A single moment of appreciation can turn an average member into a lifelong leader. Even they might become your successors in the leadership ladder.

Many LOs once flourished but are now struggling—even to send the annual subscription fees. Why? No leaders. And when there are no leaders, the blame falls on one person—the past leader who never built successors.

Great leaders don't just lead; they create more leaders. Look at your term. Who are you mentoring? Who is stepping up? If your team cannot run without you, you've failed—not as a President, but as a leader.

So, next time you hold an event, don't just celebrate the success. Celebrate the people. Recognize contributions, reward efforts, and plant the seeds for future leadership. Because leadership isn't about how great *you* were—it's about how many great leaders you left behind.

And who knows? Maybe the person you appreciate today will be standing in your shoes tomorrow. That's when you know you've truly led.

Update and Upgrade

Imagine using a 2005 Nokia phone today. No WhatsApp, no UPI, no Instagram. Just that nostalgic *Snake* game. Fun? Maybe for a day. Useful? Absolutely not.

Now, apply the same logic to leadership. If you don't update and upgrade, you become obsolete.

The world is evolving at lightning speed. Leadership styles that worked a decade ago might not work today. Gone are the days when PR and marketing meant physically meeting people, distributing pamphlets, and manually driving event participation. Now, everything reaches people's hands in seconds—yet leaders still struggle to bring in participation!

And here's the irony: despite having social media, WhatsApp, and AI-powered marketing, leaders still lament, "Even though I call people one-on-one, they don't turn up!" Déjà vu? Well, refer to Chapter 9—Not everyone likes Biryani! No matter how much effort you put in, some people just won't show up. Instead of complaining, use technology smartly—automate reminders, engage through interactive content, and focus on those who are actually interested.

Think of yourself as a smartphone. You need software updates. A leader running on outdated thoughts is like an old mobile OS—eventually, nothing will be compatible with you. People will stop syncing with your ideas. New members won't connect with your approach. And before you know it, you're stuck in the past, wondering why no one listens to you anymore.

Upgrading doesn't mean forgetting traditions—it means evolving them. Technology is not your enemy—it's your secret weapon. A good leader embraces new tools, learns new skills, and stays ahead of the curve.

So, the next time you hit "Remind me later" on a software update, remember—leaders who postpone their upgrades eventually crash.

Smile, laugh and let go!

At the end of the day, you are just a sand particle in the ocean of galaxies. Yes, really. While you are losing sleep over a WhatsApp committee fight, the universe is busy expanding. So, relax! Don't take life too seriously—you won't get out alive anyway.

A good friend once took a bus trip to Munnar, a breathtaking hill station. The ticket was ₹45, and he handed over ₹50. The conductor promised ₹5 change later. And guess what? Instead of soaking in the misty hills and stunning tea plantations, this guy spent the entire 2-hour journey fixated on that missing ₹5 —completely blind to the priceless views outside!

Many Presidents carry stress like a badge of honor. Meetings, targets, politics—loading their 1.5 kg brain with so much tension that even AI would refuse to process it. But tell me this—will people remember your stress, your ego, or your achievements? Nope. They'll remember how you made them feel.

I always had one wish—a traffic jam at my funeral! Not because I troubled people while alive, but because I touched their lives so much that they all came to say goodbye. If you want the same, drop your ego.

Your vision and values must be bigger than your ego. Leadership isn't about winning arguments—it's about winning hearts. If you can make people smile, laugh, and feel valued, you've already succeeded.

Don't let small things steal your peace. A few words from someone shouldn't haunt your entire day. People will talk —about your work, your personal life, even your haircut! Let them. You focus on the journey. Every moment, every experience is a lesson. Observe, learn, and move on. In the recent movie, Lucky Bhaskar (2024), I loved this dialogue, *"A 30-minute hurt isn't worth a 24-hour bad mood!"*

Laugh often, even at yourself. Celebrate small victories. Crack jokes in meetings. Make leadership fun. Stress, politics, and conflicts will always be there, but so will the choice to not let them consume you.

Because in the end, it's simple— live your life in a way that even death feels like a standing ovation.

Don't compare

If you really want to be happy, here's a golden rule—stop comparing yourself to others. Seriously. Someone will always be richer, smarter, or have a better hairline than you. If you keep looking at others, you'll spend your whole life feeling behind. Instead, compare yourself to who you were yesterday. Just focus on getting 1% better every day.

Sounds small? Let's do the math (don't worry, I'll keep it simple). If you improve by just 1% daily, in a year, you'll be 37 times better than where you started! That's compound interest on self-improvement. But the catch? Consistency.

But most people treat life like a 100-meter race—always looking left and right, trying to outrun someone else. Here's the truth: There's no finish line. The only real race is against yourself. Your laziness. Your procrastination. Your fear of failure. And if you're improving, you've already won.

So, don't stress about who's ahead or behind. Focus on small, consistent progress. Master one new skill. Read one page extra. Smile one more time. That's how real success happens—not overnight, but bit by bit, day by day.

Don't chase someone else's definition of success. Just get better. Every single day.

Because in the end, that's what JCI has as its tagline—Be Better!

My Support System

A huge thanks to the two Devi in my life—Abinaya Devi (my wife) and Muthu Vijaya Devi (my sister)—for their unwavering support (even if it came with a few sighs and eye-rolls) during my endless JCI travels.

Muthuvel (my ever-composed brother-in-law), your quiet strength and calm presence have been a rock-solid support system.

Arya (my little boss), Jaisha (the ever-curious niece), and Aadhvik (the nephew with a sharp memory)—you all have put up with my absences and still welcomed me back without demanding too many bribes.

Your love and patience, whether expressed loudly or through subtle hints, have fueled this book. If you ever wonder why this book exists, just know—you all played a part in making it happen!

Let us stay CONNECTed!

Got questions? Want to share your thoughts about the book? Or just want to say hi? Kindly scan the QR code below to reach me on WhatsApp!

Feel free to visit my website:
www.connectmurali.com to know more about me!

Interested in JCI?

If this book has sparked your interest in leadership and growth, JCI is the place to be!

Connect with JFS Saravana Kumar P. the Zone President for 2025, (Zone 18, JCI India) to learn more about how you can be a part of this amazing journey.

Let's grow, lead, and create an impact together!